Assertiveness For Teens

4 Easy to Use Methods to Stop Bullying and Stand Up for Yourself

By

Maria Van Noord

book.

By reading this document, the reader agrees that under no circumstances is the author responsible for any losses, direct or indirect, which are incurred as a result of the use of information contained within this document, including, but not limited to, — errors, omissions, or inaccuracies.

Table of Contents

Chapter: 01 Types of Communication

Assertiveness is an empowering personality trait that allows you to stand up for your own, and other people's, rights. Assertiveness is congruent with fighting for what is right in a calm and non-aggressive manner. The biggest power of an assertive person is his or her ability to articulate even the most conflicting ideas without upsetting or antagonizing the opposing party.

The quality of assertiveness is to stand up firmly for your rights by expressing your feelings, thoughts, and beliefs in honest, direct, and non-aggressive ways. It is important to note that assertiveness includes deep sensitivity for the thoughts, beliefs, and feelings of other people. Assertiveness is typically seen as a balance between passive and aggressive behaviors.

Since assertiveness is connected to communication and behaviors, it will help to know the different communication styles that exist to improve the understanding of assertiveness better. Here are the primary types of communication:

1. Passive
2. Aggressive
3. Assertive
4. Passive-Aggressive

Let us look at each type in a little detail, along with some examples.

PASSIVE COMMUNICATION

People with a passive style of communication tend not to express their feelings, opinion, and thoughts openly. They are not equipped to fight for their rights. Passive communication is typically associated with low self-esteem. Based on their belief that they are not worth taking care of, passive communicators do not respond overtly to angry or hurtful situations.

Instead, they unwittingly accumulate negative feelings and resentment. But, one can only collect and hold so much negativity. Therefore, such people are prone to emotional outbursts when their threshold levels are breached.

PASSIVE COMMUNICATORS

- Do not assert themselves even when they know they should
- Allow others to infringe on their rights
- Do not express their opinions and needs
- Nearly always speak in an apologetic tone
- Exhibit slumped body posture and do not maintain eye contact

All these actions or inactions result in feelings of depression, inadequacy, immaturity, and confusion. Passive communication is good at times, especially when you are required to show deference to people better qualified and more knowledgeable than you. However, if it is your default mode of communication, then silence is not golden.

EXAMPLES OF HOW A PASSIVE COMMUNICATOR WOULD TALK AND BEHAVE:

- I am not able to fight off that bully
- I am not smart enough to clear the test
- I am not worthy of being in the school basketball team
- None of my friends care for me

CHALLENGES OF PASSIVE COMMUNICATION:

- People will disregard your needs and opinions
- You will easily be passed up for promotions and other good offers
- You will build unnecessary stress
- You expect others to be able to read your mind
- Can lead to an aggressive communication style in a very

dangerous way

- You will most likely end up being a bully or a bully's side-kick
- Have you ever heard of great leaders of the world who have this style of communication? Never!

AGGRESSIVE COMMUNICATION

If passive communicators are at one end of the communication spectrum, then aggressive communicators are at the opposite end. Aggressive communicators express their opinions and feelings so strongly that it violates the rights of others around them.

AGGRESSIVE COMMUNICATORS

- Dominate others
- Humiliate people to control them
- Attack, criticize and blame others
- Speak in demanding and loud voices
- Act rudely or threateningly
- Are bad listeners
- Are frequent interrupters
- Maintain an overbearing posture and piercing eye contact

EXAMPLES OF HOW AGGRESSIVE COMMUNICATORS TALK AND BEHAVE:

- I am right, and you are wrong
- I am superior to you
- I can infringe upon your rights
- I will get my way, no matter what
- Everything is your fault
- You owe me

CHALLENGES OF AGGRESSIVE COMMUNICATORS:

- If you are a default aggressive communicator, you are going to be:
- Alienated by your friends and peers
- No one will want to be identified with you
- You will generate hatred and fear among your friends; consequently, you will remain friendless
- You will always find external circumstances and other people to blame for your failures, because of which you will never be able to grow and mature

Aggressive leaders from history have always been referred to as ruthless. Here are a few classic examples:

Genghis Khan – Although he is credited with uniting the Mongol tribes into a powerful single country which succeeded in conquering nearly the whole of China, his methods are considered brutal. He is known to have slaughtered and plundered civilians thoughtlessly and ruthlessly.

Queen Mary I – Also referred to as Bloody Mary, she was the only child of King Henry VIII and Catherine of Aragon. In an attempt to restore Catholicism in England, she gave orders to burn hundreds of Protestants at the stake.

Joseph Stalin – To bring about rapid collectivization and industrialization in the 1930s in the USSR, Stalin imprisoned millions of workers in labor camps, starved them, carried out the 'Great Purge' of the intelligentsia, armed forces, and the government in his country.

A common denominator of such aggressive leaders is the fact that they were willing to do anything to achieve what they believed was right with utter disregard for everyone and everything else.

PASSIVE-AGGRESSIVE COMMUNICATION

People who have developed the passive-aggressive style of communication seem passive on the surface but are, in truth, showing anger subtly and indirectly.

Have you seen Prisoners-of-War (POWs) behaving in movies? Most of them are characterized as showing this behavior because of the overwhelming feeling of helplessness combined with simmering rage. POWs are often characterized by the way they mock the enemy or indulge in some behind-the-scene act of sabotage.

Alternatively, how have you behaved with your parents when they try to discipline? Muttering something nasty under your breath while following their instructions half-heartedly? That is another example of passive-aggressive communication.

PASSIVE-AGGRESSIVE COMMUNICATORS:

- Mutter under their breath instead of confronting the issue or person
- Do not acknowledge their anger openly
- Their body language and their feelings are mismatched; they could be smiling when they are actually angry
- Employ sarcasm frequently
- Appear to cooperate but try to sabotage in an underhanded way

EXAMPLES OF HOW PASSIVE-AGGRESSIVE COMMUNICATORS TALK AND BEHAVE:

- I frustrate and sabotage because I am weak and helpless
- I do not know how to beat your scores through hard work and so I will find ways to cheat and get better scores
- I will look as if I am cooperating, but I resent the situation I am in

CHALLENGES OF PASSIVE-AGGRESSIVE COMMUNICATORS:

- They remain stuck in positions of helplessness, just like the POWs
- They will be able to vent off resentment through stealth, although real issues never get addressed
- They become alienated from people around them

EXAMPLES OF PASSIVE-AGGRESSIVE BEHAVIORS IN SCHOOL:

The teacher has given orders to sit quietly and work out 10 Math problems. There will typically be at least a few students who will do everything but sit silently at their desks. They could be performing seemingly innocuous tasks, such as sharpening their pencils with the needless ruckus, rubbing their eyes and yawning loudly, asking for a restroom break, or some such thing.

Students deliberately underperform to exhibit their passive-aggressive behavior to their teachers. They will scribble their assignments and make it impossible for their teacher to read and grade them. They will deliberately give wrong answers, despite knowing the right ones.

ASSERTIVE COMMUNICATION

Assertive communication is one in which people clearly state and expresses their opinions and needs without hurting or violating the rights of other people. They are firm and yet do not exhibit aggression of any sort.

Malala Yousufzai, a Pakistani activist for women's education, became the youngest Nobel Prize laureate when she won the Nobel Peace Prize in 2014. She literally challenged and overcame the fear of death to stand up for her right to education, even as she was shot and left for dead by terrorists. She said, "I raised my voice not so that I can shout but so that people without a voice can be heard."

Millie Bobby Brown is a teenage sensation who plays the role of a mysterious girl in the famous sci-fi series, Stranger Things. She says, "I am a strong person. Even if people say something horrible about me, I just respond with, 'Ok, whatever,' and continue being me."

Assertiveness is closely related to high self-esteem.

ASSERTIVE COMMUNICATORS

- Express their needs and opinions appropriately, clearly, and respectfully
- Take responsibility for their actions
- Communicate with everyone with dignity and respect
- Are in control of their emotions
- Speak in a calm and relaxed tone of voice
- Maintain a relaxed body posture
- Are competent and in control of the situation
- Do not allow people to manipulate and abuse them
- Stand up firmly for their rights

EXAMPLES OF HOW ASSERTIVE COMMUNICATORS TALK AND BEHAVE:

- We are all equally entitled to our rights, opinions, and feelings

- I am confident of myself
- I know that I have choices in my life, and I must weigh the pros and cons and make the correct choices for my life
- I speak honestly and clearly
- I don't beat around the bush; I state my case to the point
- I will stand up for my rights and will not allow them to be violated by anyone
- I respect and honor the rights of other people

EFFECTS OF BEING AN ASSERTIVE COMMUNICATOR:

- You will be respected by your friends and peers
- You will address core issues in your life, which will help you to grow and mature as an individual.
- As you create a friendly environment to include everyone, you will always be well-liked and popular

Nearly every great leader of the world has been able to exhibit his or her assertiveness. Here are some classic examples, whose behaviors you can emulate right from your teenage years, which will hold you in good stead all through your life:

Abraham Lincoln – Known for his calm and composed demeanor, Abraham Lincoln was an amazing communicator who never offended anyone with his superiority. He was basically a quiet man except when the need to stand up for rights was there. Then, he would stand tall and firm, and fight openly, honestly, and without violating the rights of others.

Rosa Parks – This civil rights movement leader was the epitome of quiet assertiveness. Although not very outspoken, she did not hesitate to do what was right, even in the face of hostility.

Assertiveness helps us take care of ourselves and our needs and is an essential ingredient for a happy and healthy life. There is a general acceptance that men are naturally more assertive than women. This general outlook enhances the pressure on both girls and boys to learn and master assertiveness for the following reason:

- Girls – because they have to work harder than boys to become assertive

Boys – because they have to live up to the standards expected by society.

The good thing about assertiveness is that it can be imbibed by anyone with a little practice, patience, and diligence. In fact, those who don't try to learn the art of assertiveness will be at a big disadvantage in today's highly competitive world.

Chapter: 02 Why Do We Behave the Way We Do?

Why do people behave the way they do? What drives them? Why are some people aggressive to the point of hurting others while others are passive-aggressive and pretend to do one thing while wanting the exact opposite? In modern culture, we are conditioned to believe that suppressing or not expressing your feelings and emotions is the best way to handle them.

Nothing can be farther from the truth considering that emotions, along with intellect and other mechanisms, are used by us to understand what is happening to us and around us. In fact, emotions give us the energy to come to terms with the various ups and downs in our lives.

The human body works best when it is in homeostasis, which is a balanced state. When we inhale, we are out of balance, and when we exhale, the balanced state is restored. Similarly, our mind goes out of balance when emotions find their way into our system, and unless there is an exit for those feelings, we continue to remain in an unbalanced state. Our system cannot be in a state of homeostasis if these emotions are not discharged from our body completely without leaving trace remnants too.

Expressing our feelings is the best form of exit for our emotions. If we continue to allow our feelings to accumulate inside us instead of expressing them, they will build pressure in our system, which is called the 'percolator effect' in psychology. A percolator is an old-fashioned coffee-brewing machine that builds pressure inside through heating so that coffee is brewed.

Similarly, if emotions, which are nothing but forms of energy, are not released, the pressure inside you is going to build up. When it crosses a certain threshold (which is dependent on the individual's capability to hold such pressures), it will burst forth in nasty ways, including in the form of physical pain such as stomachache, gastritis, ulcers, etc. Of course, the most common way of expressing such repressed emotions is to demonstrate it on family and loved ones by screaming, yelling, and even physical abuse.

While some people bring out repression in aggressive ways, others use passive-aggressive methods. As discussed in Chapter 1, aggressive behavior takes on the form of physical abuse, yelling, and screaming; passive-aggressive behavior comes in the form of cursing under the breath, deliberately underperforming, etc.

So, every time you get angry or frustrated or upset about something and you don't find a healthy way to engage with these emotions and release the energy from your system, the emotional pressure is bound to build and end up in nasty situations for you. While your aggressive behavior has bad outcomes for the victim, it results in even worse results for you.

Let us look at some of the reasons, along with examples of aggressive and passive-aggressive behavior. Many times, the causes for your negative emotions might be beyond your control; however, you must remember how you respond to these problems is entirely in your control.

REASONS FOR AGGRESSIVE AND PASSIVE-AGGRESSIVE BEHAVIORS IN TEENAGERS

Numerous studies have been conducted and multiple reasons have emerged as to why teenagers behave aggressively. Some of the reasons include:

Trauma – Illness or death of a loved one, extreme harassment by parents or siblings, ongoing discords and fights between parents or divorce are all highly stressful situations. Teenagers are not mature enough to handle such pressures well. Instead, they become aggressive.

Ingrid Bergman, one of the most captivating stars of Hollywood, had a very troubled childhood. Her mother died when she was 3 years old, and her father died when she was a teenager. She was forced to live with an uncle who was against her wanting to become an actress. A classic case for aggressive behavior! And yet, she rose above the challenges and became one of the most exotic actresses the world has ever seen.

Abuse – Sexual, mental, or physical abuse is another common reason for aggressive behavior amongst teenagers. The abuse angers the children, and yet they feel helpless against older and stronger people. It is also not easy to find someone trusting to talk about such things with. So, their emotions pile up inside and aggression is their way out.

Rita Hayworth, the famous glamorous actress, and dancer of the 20th century had a very troubled adolescence because of her extremely demanding father. He pushed her unreasonably hard to achieve success. While she did achieve success, her adolescence is sure to have been very, very difficult.

Peer Pressure – Puberty is a very difficult time for most teenagers. Raging hormones wreak havoc on the body and mind. Weight gain, freckles, and other forms of physical awkwardness make teenagers the butt of jokes and victims of bullying. Sometimes, wanting to belong and being rejected creates stress for young people. Such situations also drive aggressive behavior.

Janis Joplin is, perhaps, one of the most famous and popular rock stars of the 20th century. Her most turbulent period was her teenage years. Puberty kicked in and she gained weight. She was the butt of all ridicule and humiliation in school and among her peers. She had to fight her way out of it. It was only when Janis came into contact with like-minded people who shared her interest in music and singing that she found her peace with life. Of course, after that, there was nothing to stop her growth.

Addiction and Abuse – Adolescence is a very vulnerable age. Peer pressure and the desire to 'fit in' drives many teenagers to try drugs and alcohol. After a certain point, many of them become addicted to these items, and aggression is one of the most common negative effects of addiction.

Low Self-Esteem – This is, perhaps, one of the most important reasons for teenagers becoming aggressive. Many teenagers are victims of low self-esteem due to multiple reasons, including emotional conflicts, stressful academic pressures, high parental expectations, and more. They exhibit aggressive behavior to cover up their low self-esteem.

Don't panic if you are a teenager showing aggressive behavior. The good thing about aggressive behavior in teenagers is that it is very easy to manage and overcome because you are still young, and you have time and energy on your side to learn to become masters of your emotions instead of being under control of your feelings.

EXAMPLES OF AGGRESSIVE TEENAGERS WHO TURNED OUT REALLY WELL IN ADULT LIFE

Jay Z – This famous musician, rapper, and producer were arrested when he was 16 for carrying crack. A very inspiring quote from him: "The way to redemption is not to run away

23

from your error-ridden past but to understand and learn from the mistakes and build a strong future."

Charles Sutton – This famous actor was arrested and convicted for manslaughter when he was 17. He even attacked a guard in jail. He turned around when he found a purpose in his life: to become an actor. He says, "I used to be a hard-hearted person. However, once I decided to change, many good things started happening."

Dwayne Johnson – This successful wrestler with a highly successful film career admitted to being arrested 8 or 9 times by the time he was 16. Today, he only remembers thinking of a firm resolution he made to himself the last time he was arrested: that he would do everything in his power not to let it happen in his life again.

Stephen Fry – One of Britain's biggest stars of all time, Stephen Fry was arrested for credit card fraud when he was 17. His life turned around after he completed his sentencing. This man returned to college and devoted himself entirely to his studies. In his autobiography, Stephen Fry says, "I used to feel the working of my heart and lungs thumping energy through my entire body. I felt the enormity of real, human power I possessed; the power to strive and endure continuously."

SOME INTERESTING POINTERS TO PASSIVE-AGGRESSIVE BEHAVIORS

Why do some people use passive aggression instead of direct aggression? Please remember that the effects and outcomes of both behaviors are the same; emotions are not handled effectively and healthily in both cases. Yet, passive aggression is seen more commonly than direct aggression. Here are a few reasons for that:

Direct anger is not whereas sugar-coated anger is accepted in society – We have always been taught to hide anger because it is a socially unaccepted emotion. However, you are allowed to put up a fight in a 'nice sugar-coated' way. So, we put on a show of not being angry by using subversive means of releasing the emotion through underhand dealings, or muttering under our breath or seeking revenge indirectly, etc.

It is easy to rationalize passive-aggression – For example, suppose your dad told you to clean your room. You get angry first, then you pout, then you procrastinate, and finally, on repeated persistence, you simply take everything lying around in your room and shove it under your bed. Now, your dad is furious. You quickly rationalize by saying, "I don't see why you're so angry. I was planning to clean up after studying for my exams." Alternatively, you might say, "No matter what I do, you always find fault." And your poor dad does not know how to respond.

See how easy it is to rationalize passive-aggression and put the other person on the defensive?

Revenge is sweet – Passive aggression is all about taking revenge in a round-about way, and revenge is undoubtedly sweet; all the more if the avenger gets it with social acceptance! You are tired after a hectic day at school, and you want your father to stop nagging (or so you think) you about cleaning your room. So, you shove everything under the bed knowing very well he is going to fume! That look of helpless rage when you gave that almost perfect but hollow excuse of wanting to clean it after studying for your exams was sweet, wasn't it?

Regardless of these reasons, passive aggression is not an effective way of handling and releasing emotional energy. The most effective way of handling emotion is through assertiveness; letting people know your opinions and emotions in a firm but gentle way without hurting other people's feelings.

Chapter: 03 Current Level of Assertiveness

Let us start by gauging your current level of assertiveness with a simple questionnaire based on a self-expression scale taken from the academic literature produced under the title The College Self-Expression Scale (by John P. Galassi & others) published in 1974.

Questionnaire to Gauge the Current Level of Assertiveness for Teenagers

These questions are worded to prompt a 'yes' or a 'no' answer from you. At the end of it, you will be able to see what level of assertiveness you are at, and which areas you need to improve on. The more Yeses, the more assertive you are.

Q1. Suppose you are standing in line along with 10 other students to submit an application form at the school office. Now, someone new comes and goes straight to the office to hand over his or her application form without even glancing at the line of students patiently waiting to do the same thing. Will you raise your voice? Y/N

Q2. You shopped for a pair of sneakers at a big departmental store located quite a distance away from your home. When you came home, you realized they were slightly defective. Will you take the trouble to go back and get them exchanged? Y/N

Q3. You had a huge argument with your friend regarding a particular assignment to be done jointly with her or him. The friend finally gave in to your argument, and both of you submitted it the way you insisted on your friend's suggestion. However, your teacher returned it, asking that the assignment be redone in precisely the same way your friend had suggested. Will you apologize to your friend for your mistake? Y/N

Q4. If you are angry with your parents for any reason, do you always tell them in an honest and upfront way about your feelings, along with the reasons for the anger? Y/N

Q5. Your best friend borrowed some money from you about a month ago saying he would return it to you when he received his next pocket money. You know that his parents have already given him his pocket money. Will you remind him to return your money? Y/N

Q6. When you are talking to other people including friends, teachers, and family members, are you sensitive to their feelings when you respond to them or discuss things that you know will affect their emotions? Y/N

Q7. Continuing from Q6, do you make an effort to say what you have to say without hurting them but without being overly sensitive to their feelings? Y/N

Q8. If you need a favor from a friend, do you ask for it openly without feeling uncomfortable? Y/N

Q9. You are on your first date with a boy/girl whom you worked very hard to get. The dinner at the restaurant is not to their satisfaction. Will you let the waiter know your feelings, even at the risk of coming across as picky and choosy in front of your date? Y/N

Q10. You walk into a garment shop, and you simply love the red dress on the mannequin. The salesman also says wonderful things about the dress. However, you know it is very pricey and you cannot afford it. Would you stand your ground and say no to the salesman and not feel uncomfortable about it? Y/N

Q11. You are studying for an upcoming important exam. Suddenly a group of friends drop in to chat and generally chill out with you. Will you politely tell them to return at a more convenient time? Y/N

Q12. Do you feel comfortable sharing opinions with your peers and siblings?

Q13. Do you feel comfortable sharing opinions with your parents?

Q14. Do you feel comfortable sharing opinions with your teachers and other elders in your life?

Q15. You are in a history class. History is your favorite subject, and the teacher is your favorite too. The teacher suddenly says something that you know to be incorrect. Will you stand up and correct the teacher? Y/N

Q16. Your dad's boss, whom you have met before and are very fond of, comes home to dinner one day and says something that you strongly disagree with. Will you make an effort to present the countering viewpoint?

Q17. You went to a store and bought something and walked out. On the way home, you realize that you were short-changed. Would you walk back and request to be given the right amount back? Y/N

Q18. A really good friend, from whom you have taken help to do your Math assignments because you are weak in the subject, comes to you with an unreasonable request. Will you be able to refuse politely? Y/N

Q19. One of your most loved uncles is behaving in a very annoying way recently. Will you find a way to tell him politely that his behavior is not nice? Y/N

Q20. Suppose you are playing a game with some junior players. You and your friend are experts in this particular sport. However, the junior players are very skilled, and it looks like they are going to win the match. Suddenly you notice your friend sneakily indulging in a cheating act, which will result in you winning the match. Will you own up to what happened and concede defeat? Y/N

Q21. You shared a very deep secret with your best friend, and he betrays your confidence by spreading the secret around. He is not only your best friend but also a very popular guy at school. Will you stand up and tell him you are disappointed with him and want nothing to do with him anymore? Y/N

Q22. You are standing in line at a departmental store to bill the items you have purchased. The billing clerk attends to a person who came after you. Will you bring this unfair act to the attention of the store manager? Y/N

Q23. You desperately need some money. Are you comfortable asking your friend to help? Y/N

Q24. You are a fairly good sport and can take jokes on

yourself quite well. However, a good friend has gone a bit overboard teasing you, and you are not feeling nice about it. Will you stand up and tell your friend your feelings? Y/N

Q25. You have arrived late for an important meeting. Will you have the courage to walk up to the front row and take a seat, even if this action draws attention to you? Before answering, remember you have the option of sitting inconspicuously at the back. Y/N

Q26. You are engaged in a conversation with a friend, and an important person (perhaps, someone of good social standing) interrupts your conversation. Will you tell the person to excuse you until you finish the current conversation? Y/N

Q27. Someone is unjustly finding fault with you. Can you tactfully express your disagreement? Y/N

Q28. Do you believe you are comfortable being assertive? Y/N

Look at the 'No' answers, and explore the situation again, and see what it takes for you to reconsider the answer. Do you need to reprogram your thinking process to make yourself more assertive in the given situation? What are the causes of your behavior? Can you connect anything personal to that particular behavior that is preventing you from being assertive? What changes can you bring about in yourself to be more assertive?

MAINTAIN AN ASSERTIVENESS JOURNAL

For about two weeks, maintain an assertiveness journal in which you make daily entries. Note down each incident when you could have shown assertiveness. It could be discussions, unfair practice, bullying, someone cheating on a test, or anything else. Make a note of the following elements:

- Did you voice your opinion?
- How did you talk?
- What were the emotions going through your mind?
- Did you think you managed the emotions easily enough and remained calm and composed, or were you struggling?
- Did your ability to manage your emotions affect the result? If yes, how?
- Did you believe you could have handled the discussion in a better way? Were you happy with the outcome or was the other party happy? Did you dwell excessively on the outcome of the discussion?

These are only pointers. Make a note of all the relevant things that you know affected the outcome. Don't judge yourself while making the entries. Remember you are in the process of learning. Now, at the end of two weeks, read through your journal and see if you can pick out triggers that drove your behavior in any particular way. Can you see a pattern in your behavior?

If you are unsure of making objective observations, show your journal to a trusted friend, and discuss with him or her openly and honestly. You can arrive at your current level of assertiveness using the information from these diary entries.

GET TO KNOW YOUR CURRENT COMMUNICATION STYLE

Choose the most appropriate answer that matches your current communication level. Be honest. Otherwise, there is no value in this exercise. Everyone is struggling to improve themselves.

Q1. Someone gets ahead of you while you are in line. What do you do?

1. Give them the benefit of the doubt and tell them gently that you were waiting before them
2. Glare at them angrily while saying nothing, and push them 'accidentally' to take your rightful place
3. Say and do nothing
4. Express your displeasure firmly and tell them to go back to their place

Q2. You are meeting your friend to do your class project together. You came on time, and your friend arrived nearly 30 minutes late. What do you do?

1. You rudely tell your friend you don't like to be kept waiting for so long
2. Say nothing because you don't like conflict
3. Look at your watch, and ask your friend for an explanation for the delay
4. Say nothing because you left after waiting for 10 minutes

Q3. Your friend constantly makes you the butt of all his jokes in class. You have already told him that his attitude hurts you. But he has not relented. What do you do?

1. Decide to build a thicker skin so that you don't feel bad about these jokes
2. Re-evaluate the value of this friendship in your life, and do the needful to get out
3. Start making your friend the butt of your own jokes, matching each joke of his with your own veiled attack
4. Don't talk about jokes again, but bring up topics that you know anger and annoy your friend
5. Gauging your current level of assertiveness arms you with the relevant information needed to take corrective measures in building and strengthening your assertiveness level.

Chapter: 04 BUILDING ASSERTIVENESS BASED ON YOUR CORE VALUES

Core or personal values are qualities or traits that you don't just consider worthwhile, but which form the fundamental driving force of your life. Personal core values guide your life choices and behaviors. If you get your core values right, then you will be able to make swift and focused decisions that are aligned with your life purpose.

THE ELEMENTS THAT DEFINE CORE VALUES

There are primarily three elements that define core values, including:

1. *Theoretically, you should be able to live by them irrespective of your physical condition* – For example, honesty is a core value that can be lived by you no matter where you are. You could be stuck in a little prison cell, and even then remain honest. However, if your core value was physical fitness, then it might not be possible to live by it at all times and in all places. Therefore, being athletic or being physically fit

37

cannot really be a core value.

2. ***There is no need for participation or approval from anyone else but you*** – The entire world could turn against you. But you should still be able to live by your chosen core value. For example, if courage is a core value, then you don't need anyone's approval or participation to be courageous. However, popularity requires the approval and participation of other people. Therefore, courage can be a core value whereas popularity cannot.

3. ***You should be able to apply them internally and externally simultaneously*** – This means you should be able to live by and act on the core value for yourself and for those around you together without sacrificing anyone, including yourself. This point is best explained with an illustration. For example, being a martyr cannot be a valued principle or behavior because hurting yourself for the sake of others means you are not being compassionate to yourself.

IMPORTANCE OF CORE VALUES

Your core values help you choose your relationships, your friendships, your career path, and more. Core values help you manage your energy, time, and money resources sensibly and wisely. You can focus the use of these resources productively in the direction of your core values.

Your core values give you a personal code of conduct, which helps you stay on your chosen life path even in the face of adversity. When you consistently honor your core values, you are bound to achieve a sense of fulfillment. If you don't have a set of core values or fail to follow one that you have given yourself, you are likely to fall into bad habits and regress into behaviors that are misaligned with your life purpose. When you realize your personal core values, your behavior undergoes change.

And finally, core values are very important to build your level of assertiveness. They are the guiding factors that tell you when to stand your ground, and when it is okay to let go. Core values help you with the following:

Help you make good decisions - Core values become the basis of your decision-making. They guide you to make the right choices. The absence of core values will make you uncertain about the choices you make and make you feel less assertive than required.

Help you remain confident and centered – Doing the 'right' thing will be easy if you don't have an overreaching set of guiding principles in the form of your core values. Core values help you analyze facts, emotions, and circumstances, upon which you can do the 'right' thing on a consistent basis which, in turn, builds confidence while keeping you grounded and centered.

Identifying your core values, therefore, is the cornerstone of building and growing your assertiveness.

DISCOVERING YOUR CORE VALUES

As a teenager, it is quite likely that you still haven't formed your core values. Here are some steps to help you personalize your values for yourself:

Firstly, create a list of personal values. There are more than 400 values that you can choose from, including love, acceptance, justice, temperance, prudence, ambition, friendship, respect, fun, health, responsibility, balance, health, and lots, lots more.

However, avoid going by any pre-determined list of core values. Core values make sense when you discover them from your life experiences instead of inventing them from a list constructed by someone else. Here are some pointers to help you discover your core values:

Recall your peak experiences – Think back to a moment in your life when your experience felt truly meaningful. A peak experience is something we don't ever forget. Spend some time to list 2-3 such experiences in your life. Answer the following questions regarding those experiences:

- Describe the event or experience.
- What were the feelings in your mind?
- What was going on in your mind?

- What were the values that you were committing to yourself at that time? It could have been unwitting at that time. However, now when you recall those experiences, those values will stand out.

Recall your worst experiences – Now, in the same way, recall a couple of the worst experiences, and as above, write down answers to the same set of questions, except the last question will be: "What were the values that you were suppressing?"

Define your code of conduct – After your basic human needs including food, clothing, and shelter are met, what are the next most important elements of life that you must necessarily have to achieve fulfillment and make your life meaningful. Here are some examples:

- A sense of adventure and excitement
- Creativity
- Health and vitality
- Learning new things
- Beauty of nature

Primarily, what are those personal values without which your life simply withers away? Or what are those personal values without which you might live but never thrive?

Combine similar values together from your list – Take the list of values you get from the above experiences and categorize similar values together if the list is long and unwieldy. For example, timeliness, accountability, and responsibility can be clubbed together. Development, learning, and growth can all be combined.

Identify the theme of each group of values – For example, timeliness, accountability, and responsibility can be grouped as discipline and development; learning, and growth can be categorized as learning and growth.

Take the top 5 from this set of core values – Again, if you are still left with a big list, take the top 4-5 core values that are essential for life. Use your answers to the following questions to help you:

- What values are absolutely necessary for your life?
- What values reflect your life path?
- What values are needed to be content and happy?

Ideally, the number of your core values should be somewhere between 5 and 10. If it is less, then you could risk leaving out critical elements of your life. If the list of your core values is very long, remembering and keeping track of them might prove to be difficult.

And finally, rank your core values in order of importance. This last step could be the most challenging part of setting up your core values. Take some time and do your ranking. Sleep on it and recheck to see if you have conflicts. Rearrange the ranking if required. Persist until you are completely sure of your core values and their order of importance in your life.

At this point, it makes sense to list some examples of ideas and concepts that cannot be used as core values because they don't meet one or more of the 3-element criteria mentioned above:

- Family connection – this core requires the participation of other people
- Financial security – this also requires favorable factors beyond your control
- Marriage – again, a partner's participation and approval is required
- Physical fitness or strength – this requires comparison with others, a particular physical situation, for it to be effective
- Emotional detachment – this also requires societal approval as to what is considered emotional detachment; moreover, external circumstances beyond your control could easily prevent you from living by this principle
- Travel – requires money, time, and other external resources

CORE VALUES AND ASSERTIVENESS

Once you have your core values in place and are completely engaged with it, your ability to enhance your level of assertiveness will go up a few notches.

Chapter: 05 Change Your Inner Beliefs

One of the most significant challenges to increase your assertiveness level is your own thinking. All of us are molded by conditions and thinking processes that have been ingrained in us from our childhood. As a teenager, some of your thought processes are already deeply cemented in your mind. For example, you have pre-existing thoughts about yourself, the people around you, and the world at large.

Many times, these beliefs and pre-set thoughts are a result of our own experiences, along with what has been taught to us by our parents, teachers, friends, etc. For instance, as a child, you were taught not to show negative emotions, such as anger and sadness, because you would be mocked.

This attitude might have made sense then because it was an effective way to quieten a bawling kid. However, now as a teenager, you don't need to work within the same parameters. It is perfectly alright to express negative emotions because you are now old enough to keep your feelings and expressions in reasonable check. And yet, controlled by those archaic conditions, we are still scared or disinclined to express negative emotions.

CHANGING YOUR MINDSET THAT FACILITATES ASSERTIVE BEHAVIOR

Now, as a teenager, you have to tell your mind to unlearn old and archaic conditionings and learn and master new thoughts and inner beliefs that facilitate assertive behavior. Here are some examples:

1. Staying silent works like cancer and is a trait of a coward. There is no wisdom in not standing up for your rights, opinions, and feelings. By standing up for your rights, you might not win every battle you participate in. But, everyone will know what you stood for – so said Shannon L. Adler. She is an inspirational author who has multiple bestselling books to her credit.

Therefore, don't stagnate in old valueless beliefs that are not relevant anymore. Allow your heart and mind to grow and evolve as you pass each stage of your life. Be ready to eliminate irrelevant and limiting beliefs and embrace new and forward-thinking concepts and ideas.

2. Warren Buffet, one of the most successful businessmen and global business investor of all times, says, "The primary difference between truly successful and ordinarily successful people is that

the truly successful people say NO to most of the things."

Gauge your current mindset and inner belief. Understand where you are presently and where you want to reach. Once you are clear about your purpose and core values of your life, then focus on only those things that add value to these important elements. Channelize all your energies towards this goal alone and stay away from or say NO to everything else.

For example, if your 4-year life purpose is to complete a computer science engineering course, then your entire teenage life should be focused on this target alone. Let all your energies and resources be channelized towards this one goal and change your mindset completely for this purpose. For everything else, the answer is NO.

3. Malcolm X, the American Muslim minister, and human rights activist, said, "No one can give you equality, freedom, justice, or anything else. If you are man enough, then reach out and take it."

Until you take things into your own hands and do what is needed to get justice and freedom, these elements will always be beyond your reach. As a child, many things in your life were done for you by your parents and caretakers. However, think back and you will recollect and, slowly but surely, your parents would have handed over the responsibility of things for yourself.

For example, there was a time when you literally needed to be spoon-fed. Soon, you learned to assert yourself to eat on your own. In fact, ask your parents and they will tell you that you fought to eat on your own. It is an innate survival behavior to be aggressive. Our ancestors had to be aggressive to survive.

However, as we learned to civilize ourselves, we picked up the skill of toning our aggression down to assertiveness because modern life does not need aggression. It only requires us to politely view our thoughts without infringing upon the freedom of others to view their own.

Driven by several factors (as discussed in Chapter 2), some of us retained the original aggressive spirit while others turned to passiveness or a passive-aggression style of communication. Assertiveness calls for a healthy balance between passiveness and aggression and balancing it is always a difficult thing to achieve.

Assertiveness, therefore, requires you to look within yourself, and change your mindset and inner beliefs, which will then be reflected in your outward behavior and lifestyle.

HOW TO GAUGE YOUR CURRENT INNER BELIEFS

Making changes or moving forward calls for you to understand the current status. Therefore, the first thing you must to do to change yourself is to identify your present state regarding inner beliefs. Here are some ways to help you:

Maintain thought diaries – Thoughts run amok in our heads, and remembering them is a huge challenge. Writing them down is the best way to handle this challenge. Start maintaining a diary for your unassertive thoughts, behaviors, and emotions, all of which are driven by your inner beliefs. Here is an example of entries in your thought diary, from which you can write your own journal.

Identifying emotions - Suppose you asked a friend to go with you to a party, and she said, 'No.' Dig deep into your mind and find answers to the following questions:

- What emotions did you feel?
- What was the intensity of these emotions (rate them as per your own ranking system; a classic example is from 1-10 in which 1 stands for 'least intense' and 10 stands for 'most intense.')

Identifying behavior - In this situation where you were hurt and annoyed, how did you behave? Answer the following questions:

- What did you do?
- What were the physical sensations and how intense were they?

Identifying thoughts –You felt tense, worried, and anxious. Identify your thoughts by answering the following questions:

- What were your thoughts?
- What was running through your head? Rate the intensity of these thoughts?

Some ground rules while you are answering these questions:

- Stick to facts
- Don't add your interpretations of the situation. For example: "She was rude to me," should not be an entry in your diary
- Rate the intensity of your emotions, thoughts, and physical sensations in each of these situations (the higher the intensity, the more the strength of your inner belief)

Making entries in your diary as mentioned above is the first part of this exercise. The second part consists of rating the strength of your beliefs. The higher the intensity of your thoughts, emotions, and behavior, the stronger your inner belief based on which these elements were triggered should be. Now, answer the following questions for the second part of the diary:

- Were my reactions and responses passive, aggressive, passive-aggressive or assertive?
- What was the evidence of my thoughts, emotions, and behaviors?
- Was I ignoring my rights and opinions or was I ignoring the other person involved in the situation?

- What were the other perspectives on the situation that I was missing?

As you answer these questions, you will get insights into how you could have been more assertive. Moreover, you also get a clear idea of what your inner beliefs are, from which you can work towards moving in a direction more conducive to an assertive way of thinking and living.

Here is a template for the first situation, when you asked your friend to go to a party:

PART I OF THE THOUGHT DIARY:

What emotions was I feeling? – Angry – 8 (the rating), hurt – 7

Physical sensations – Tight chest, tears in my eyes, tense, angry when I thought of my friend

What did I do? – Punched the boxing bag, cried a bit, and did not pick up her next call

What were my thoughts? – When she asked me to come to a party I didn't want to go, I went for her. She should have done the same for me. I don't think she wants to be my friend.

The intensity of these thoughts – 8

What kind of reactions are these? – Passive, because I didn't have the courage to present my feelings to her. Aggressive, when I punched the boxing bag. Passive-aggressive when I ignored her call.

PART II OF THE THOUGHT DIARY:

Was there any evidence that my thoughts and emotions were true? – No

Was there evidence that my thoughts and emotions could have been false? – Yes, she has done a lot of things in the past for me

Did I ignore anyone's rights? – Yes, I ignored my rights when I said yes to her request to go to a party when I didn't want to go. I ignored her rights when she chose to say no to me. The right I ignored is that everyone has a right to say no

Were there other perspectives that I could have missed in this situation? – Yes, she could have been tired. She might have had something really important to do which compelled her to say no to me. There were many occasions when I have also said no to her.

What could have been a more assertive kind of thinking in this situation? – My acceptance that she has a right to say no, and that her denial does not affect our relationship in any way.

What could have been a more assertive way of thinking in this situation? – I could have suggested a raincheck.

After this, rerate your emotions: Hurt – 2, Anger – 2

Use this template to create entries in your thought diary. Keep at this endeavor until you have been able to alter your inner beliefs significantly.

Chapter: 06 Communication Techniques to Practice

So, what are the communication techniques that you should practice to increase your level of assertiveness? Before we go into the details of assertive communication, let us understand the reason why everyone is not equally assertive.

Factors that influence people to communicate passively:

- Lack of self-confidence
- Excessively focused on pleasing others
- Excessively worried that their ideas and opinions will not be accepted by others
- Sensitive to criticism
- Not working on assertive communication skills

Factors that influence people to communicate aggressively:

- Overconfidence
- Focusing excessively on getting their own needs and desires fulfilled
- Not learning to consider and respect other people's opinions, needs, and ideas
- Insufficient listening skills

Factors that influence people to communicate assertively:

- The right level of self-confidence and awareness of

their own strengths and weaknesses

- Knowing that their opinions, views, and ideas, as well as those of others, matter equally
- Resilience to criticism, rejections, and other failures

TIPS TO IMPROVE ASSERTIVE COMMUNICATION

Use these all-purpose assertive phrases and sentences that work very well in most situations:

- Thank you for your time, but I am not interested.
- Thank you very much, but I'm afraid I cannot make time for that now.
- Thank you for your offer, but I need some me-time for the moment.
- Thanks, but no (accompanied by a genuine smile)
- Thank you for including me in this program, but I'm sorry, I will have to pass that up this time
- Thank you for connecting with me, but there is something more important that needs my attention right now.
- Thank you for sharing your opinion. What does the rest of the group think?
- I appreciate your love for partying. But, that really is not my cup of tea.

- That does sound good. Can I take some time to think over it?
- I am not sure right now. Can I take a couple of weeks to ponder over your request?
- This sounds very important. But I am unable to give the required attention right now. Can we discuss this thing in, say, a week's time?
- I don't appreciate your words (or tone of voice or below-the-belt comment)
- I truly appreciate your interest in my case.
- I don't agree with your perspective. This is how I see it.
- Please appreciate (or respect) my perspective too.
- I am offended by what you said.

Learn some of these statements and use them liberally in your speech. It is important, however, to remember that you must match your tone of voice, facial expressions, and body language with the words you use.

TIPS TO SHOW CONFIDENCE FOR ASSERTIVE COMMUNICATION

Practice the following stances:
- Stand up straight and make eye contact with your reflection in the mirror. This same technique will help you make eye contact during your interactions

with other people.

- Sit in a relaxed manner that exudes confidence
- Practice greeting people when you meet them for the first time. Write down greeting phrases and sentences, and practice them either on your own or with like-minded friends
- Try different clothing to see which suits your personality the best
- Practice courteousness and pleasing conversations

LISTENING SKILLS FOR ASSERTIVE COMMUNICATION

Being assertive requires you to be sensitive to other people's needs, views, and opinions. For this, you should practice listening skills so that you can listen to their perspectives, wants, and desires. Being assertive requires you to sometimes keep aside your views and concerns so that you can focus on those of the other people. Here are some tips to improve your listening skills:

Maintain eye contact with the speaker – Give your full attention to the speaker during the conversation. Avoid working on your computer or looking at your mobile phone or talking on the phone while someone is speaking to you. Maintain reasonable eye contact with the speaker.

Pay attention but remain relaxed – Pay attention to the

speaker but ensure you don't come across as tense. Remain calm and relaxed by screening out mental distractions from your mind.

Don't judge – Keep an open mind and don't judge a person based on what he or she says. Assertiveness calls for you to respect the right of everyone, including yourself, to have their own views and opinions. This element helps to improve your listening skills as well. When you keep an open mind and listen to people without judgment, it gives you room to accept their viewpoint wholeheartedly and without malice.

Don't interrupt and impose your solutions – Interrupting people while they are talking sends signals of aggressive behavior. Wrong messages that are sent include:

- What I am saying is more important than what you are trying to say
- I don't have the time or energy for your opinion
- I am more important than you are
- It doesn't matter to me what you think

All of us talk and think at different speeds. If you think and talk faster than your friend, it doesn't give you the right to expect your friend to catch up to your speed. On the contrary, assertiveness requires that you reduce your speed to ensure that the other person's right to express his or her views is not violated.

HANDLING CRITICISM FOR ASSERTIVE COMMUNICATION

There are three ways of handling criticism in an assertive manner:

1. If the criticism makes sense or there is truth in it, then agree with it., for example, if your best friend came to you and said, "Why did you have to interfere between my mother and me? You are always poking your nose into my affairs?" If you believe there is some truth in your friend's words, then the right way to respond assertively to this criticism is, "Yes, I do agree that sometimes I get too deeply involved in your affairs. However, I hope you realize the reason for that is you are my friend and I am concerned for your welfare."

2. If the criticism is a result of a mistake, don't hesitate to accept the mistake without rancor. Making a mistake does not make you a bad person. It is perfectly alright to accept your error with humility. For example, if your teacher looked at your homework and said, "What happened to you? You had to do Exercise 13D not 13C!" Your response should be, "Oops. I am so sorry, ma'am. I will resubmit my homework after making corrections."

3. If the criticism is unfounded, tell the person in no uncertain terms that you don't appreciate what is happening. For example, a classmate noticed that your jeans were too short in the morning, to which you have already responded. If he or she continues to make a big issue of it, don't hesitate to respond with something like, "What is your problem exactly? How are my short jeans affecting you in any way? I don't like your repeated reminders."

Here are some classic examples of people who failed and took a lot of criticism in the right way before they achieved success:

Milton Hershey – The man who gave us the delicious milk-chocolate treat was not an immediate hit. He failed multiple times and his products were criticized. He took all feedback given to him, went back to the drawing board, and kept trying until he perfected the delicious milk chocolate that we all love so much today.

Theodore Geisel – Famously called Dr. Seuss, Theodore Geisel was a highly popular children's author, cartoonist, animator, screenwriter, and a man of many more talents. His works were rejected 27 times by multiple publishing companies as 'pure rubbish.' The man simply refused to give up even in the face of such hurtful criticism. He persisted until he achieved success.

Stephen King – His first work was rejected a whopping 30

times before it became the legendary *Carrie*. He faced criticism after criticism for his writing. He treated every feedback in the right way, corrected his mistakes, and achieved fame in the world of writing. Today, over 350 million copies of his books have been sold the world over.

FINAL WRAP-UP TIPS

- Value yourself as well as the people around you
- Think before you say something; is it fair, just, and respectful?
- Discuss your desires and needs openly
- Remain calm and collected during the interaction
- Keep your eyes and mind open to new perspectives about yourself and the world around you
- Give praise wholeheartedly.
- Take compliments also wholeheartedly and without arrogance
- Take criticism in the right spirit, and work on it if it makes sense. If it does not make sense, simply thank the person for his or her opinion (you give them their right) and choose to ignore (you respect your right too)

And, finally, remember you don't live on an island. Human beings are social creatures and we live together in communities. We need each other to thrive in this world.

Respect this power of humankind, and your ability to build your assertiveness will get a boost.

Chapter: 07 Tools to Build Assertiveness

Body language speaks volumes about your level of assertiveness. Your sitting and standing postures, use of gestures, a simple handshake, and the way you present yourself to other people can change your communication style. For example, if your body is slouched, you come across as weak and inhibited.

Why are body language and nonverbal cues so important? Nonverbal communication is one of the primary components of communication amongst human beings. The way you sit in front of somebody communicates something to that person. Similarly, when you see someone standing in front of you, his or her standing posture communicates something to you.

In fact, body language is such a deeply ingrained aspect of our communication that people have learned to make sweeping judgments based on certain body language cues that are universally accepted across cultural and geographical barriers.

Interestingly, our nonverbal cues and body language can also affect our personality and behavior. For example, in the animal kingdom, the behavior of dominance, aggression, and control was characterized by expansion gestures. Primarily, it was observed that animals 'opened up' or featured expansive gestures like spreading out the arms or spreading out their wings (in the case of animals) or expanding the chest area to reflect dominance over others. This is true of human beings too.

Have you seen images of athletes crossing the finish line? The most common gesture is to spread out and lift their arms in the form of a V. This expansion reflects a sense of power. Contrarily, when we feel powerless, we slouch, make ourselves small by wrapping our arms around us instead of spreading them out. It is as if we don't want to bump into the person standing next to us.

Similarly, when you see two people at different power hierarchies standing next to each other, you will see that they are complementing their power gestures. For example, suppose you are standing next to your teacher because she has called you out for not submitting your assignments on time or have turned in badly done work.

Notice the way you stand; with your arms in front, and your palms joined together in a humbling kind of gesture and looking up at your teacher. Look at your teacher, and it is very likely that she is standing with her hands on her hips looking down at you.

Now, take a scenario wherein you are in a position. Suppose you are a senior pulling up a junior class student for something; you will notice that you are standing with your hands on your hips and looking down at the junior. The smaller boy or girl is looking up at you with palms held together in front.

So, in front of someone more powerful than us, we tend to take on a smaller profile, and in the presence of someone more powerful, we tend to take on a larger profile. The dominating body language is referred to as a power pose.

POWER POSES TO INCREASE ASSERTIVENESS

Research studies have proven that confident and assertive people tend to share similar mindsets as well as similar hormonal levels. Interestingly, it was observed that powerful leaders tend to have low levels of cortisol and high levels of testosterone.

Cortisol levels are associated with anxiety and stress. So, reduced levels of cortisol translate to lowered levels of stress which helps in improved anxiety management. The higher the level of testosterone, the higher the confidence level. This was observed for both men and women.

Therefore, if you have lowered cortisol level and high testosterone level, then you tend to feel confident, assertive, and very relaxed. Concurrently, you will be able to control your reactions to stressful and pressure situations. Thus, the correct level of hormones in your body can increase your level of assertiveness.

Moreover, the levels of both these hormones, namely cortisol, and testosterone, can change significantly and rapidly based on environmental, physical, and mental cues within and around you. And body language is one of those cues that can alter levels of cortisol and testosterone. Therefore, by controlling your body language, you can control your level of assertiveness and confidence.

Based on the results of various research studies, power poses were designed to help in increasing the assertiveness level. The most popular power pose is called the "Wonder Woman" pose, in which you stand erect with your hands on your hips and your head held high. This works for both men and women.

For example, if you have to get on stage to give a speech, and your level of confidence is ebbing due to stage fright, then take a couple of minutes to stand in the 'Wonder Woman' pose before going on stage. Your level of confidence will go up a few notches.

You can also make this power pose your morning routine. Every morning after you get ready to go to school, stand in the "Wonder Woman" pose for a couple of minutes. Then, leave for school feeling more refreshed, confident, and assertive than before.

MORE ASSERTIVENESS TOOLS AND TECHNIQUES

1. Visualize situations where you will stand up for your rights. For example, if you are the target of bullying, then imagine a situation in which you firmly stand up for your rights and fend off the bullies successfully. Visualizing self-assertive behaviors helps in the following ways:

- It activates the subconscious mind, resulting in the generation of creative ideas to be more assertive

- It programs your brain to recognize and receive the required resources to increase assertiveness

- It activates the law of attraction by bringing the resources, people, and other elements you will need to be more assertive.

- It increases your internal motivation to improve your assertiveness skills

2. Increase your self-awareness to become more assertive. Assertiveness is all about communication, and you cannot communicate effectively if you don't know yourself well. Therefore, get to know yourself better. Here are some tips:

- Make a list of all the negative elements in your life

including those that others see in you.

- Cross out those elements beyond your control. For example, if you have mentioned you are aging, then this element is not under your control. You simply have to accept it, like it, and learn to live with it in the best possible way. Other examples of such negative elements include death, disease, etc.

- Put a tick against those negative elements that you believe you can accept easily

- Circle those problems that you cannot accept but can control. For example, your inability to take criticism is something that you cannot accept but you can learn to overcome.

3. Love yourself. Louise Hay, the motivational author said, "Loving yourself can work many miracles in your life." If you don't love yourself first, no one else will love or respect you. Charity begins at home, and love begins with yourself. Moreover, self-love increases your assertiveness skills considerably. Here are some tips to love yourself:

- Learn ways to enjoy being alone. Starting a hobby is a great idea.

- Travel as much as you can. Seeing the world from a place other than your home can change the way you look at yourself. Moreover, traveling pushes you out of your comfort zone, and when you realize that you can have fun even when you are out of your comfort zone, your self-esteem will take a boost.

- Forgive yourself for mistakes. We all make mistakes. Don't hold old errors against yourself. Learn from the errors, forgive yourself, and move on.

- Start a journal. Writing down your emotions and thoughts will help you understand how you coped with a given situation and help you to find ways to improve upon it.

- Cut yourself some slack. Many of us are very hard on ourselves. We want to do many things and do all of them perfectly and error-free. Such a perfectionist attitude can harm you more than do you good. You will keep finding fault with everything you do, which will result in self-loathing. Therefore, stop being hard on yourself, and let yourself go at times.

- List your accomplishments. Many times, in our busy lives, we forget many of the old achievements that brought laurels to us and our loved ones. Go back to those happy times and make a list of your accomplishments. You can look at this list whenever you are in the dumps.

- Challenge yourself. Sometimes, excessive routine leads to boredom which, in turn, brings on self-loathing. Challenge yourself occasionally and get out of your comfort zone. Success will motivate you. And even if you failed, you can use the learning to get better.

4. Work on your self-esteem. Low self-esteem is one of the primary causes of low levels of assertiveness. Here are some simple tips for building self-esteem:

- Don't compare yourself with anyone else. You are unique. Love and accept yourself the way you are; warts and all.

- Identify your uniqueness and thrive in it. Albert Einstein said, "Each one of us is a genius. However, if you teach a fish to climb a tree, the poor thing will lead its life thinking it is stupid." Therefore, don't be the fish that is being taught to climb the tree. Focus on finding your ocean and become the best swimmer you were born to be.

- Don't miss out on your physical health. Multiple studies have proven the deep connection between exercising and self-esteem. Make sure you get your dose of daily exercise. Or, simply play your favorite sport every day.

- Indulge in a volunteering service. When you see other people, who are worse off than you, and you find an opportunity to help them achieve happiness, even if for a short period of time, you will feel good, and your self-esteem will get an immediate boost.

Use any of these techniques and increase your assertiveness to garner the multiple benefits it offers to you and those around you

Chapter: 08 Conclusion

Assertiveness is a powerful trait that offers multiple benefits to teenagers on the threshold of a great life. It would be naïve to not spend time and energy on building this important life skill in your adolescent years to leverage these lifelong advantages, including:

ASSERTIVE ADOLESCENTS DON'T GET BULLIED

A teenager who stands up and fights for his or her rights is not likely to get bullied. When bullies hear your confident voice saying, "Stop that right now," or "I don't like this," they are quite likely to back off. Additionally, the strength of your assertiveness could increase the resolve of other victims to stand up against bullies.

ASSERTIVE ADOLESCENTS DON'T INDULGE IN AGGRESSIVE BEHAVIOR

Verbal and physical aggression does not get anyone anywhere. In fact, such behaviors hurt the aggressor more than the victim. When you build your assertiveness skills, you don't need to show aggression because you will be able to express your opinions in a fair and open manner.

ASSERTIVE ADOLESCENTS ARE GREAT COMMUNICATORS

As an assertive teenager, you will have learned and mastered the theories of communication and why assertive behavior is the best form of communication. You will have also identified the personal core values that drive you. You know about your current level of assertiveness and what areas need improvement. You have learned the art of altering limiting beliefs that came in the way of success. You have practiced assertive communication skills, and also know other tools and techniques to build assertiveness.

Armed with all these resources (all of which are discussed in this book), you will be very well-equipped to become a great communicator. You know the right thing to do, and you know how to get it done. This oozing confidence will help you to articulately present your case, ensuring that your peers, parents, and teachers know your opinions, feelings, and views.

ASSERTIVE ADOLESCENTS HAVE HEALTHY RELATIONSHIPS

Your excellent communication skills, your ability to state your opinions firmly but gently, your respect for other people's rights, and other important traits related to assertiveness will help you maintain healthy negativity-free relationships with everyone around you. You act responsibly, you handle peer pressure prudently, and are in control of your life. Who will not like to have great relationships with such assertive people?

ASSERTIVE ADOLESCENTS HAVE HIGH SELF-ESTEEM

When you learn to speak up for yourself, your level of self-confidence will increase over time which, in turn, builds your self-esteem.

ASSERTIVE ADOLESCENTS UNDERSTAND THE POWER OF EMOTIONS

When you are assertive, it means recognize and understand the power of your emotions. You have learned to manage your feelings prudently without them taking control of your life, thereby empowering you to handle all stressful and pressure situations very well.

Now that you have a basic idea of the importance and value of assertiveness in your life, reread the book to reiterate what is being said into your psyche. As you read the book, redo the exercises, quizzes, and journal templates again so that you know exactly what you need to do to build and grow your assertiveness.

If you need more information, helpful tips, and suggestions about general motivation, confidence, self-esteem, and assertiveness, subscribe to our email list. You can also buy books specifically on Self-Esteem for Teens and Confidence for Teens by the same author.

We'll finish with this famous quote on assertiveness by Miley Cyrus, the teenage superstar: "If you believe in yourself, then anything is possible." So, believe in yourself and get ahead in life. You are born for a life of joy, happiness, and success.

CPSIA information can be obtained
at www.ICGtesting.com
Printed in the USA
LVHW021603240121
677358LV00013B/1958